Bruno's

Unplugged
Digital Minimalism for a Fulfilling Life

BS

First edition, 2024

Copyright © 2024 Bruno's

All content in this publication is licensed under the Creative Commons Attribution-NoDerivatives 4.0 International License. You are allowed to share, copy, and redistribute the material in any format or medium, provided that you give appropriate credit to the original author, do not modify the content in any way, and do not use this work for commercial purposes. For more details about the terms of this license, visit http://creativecommons.org/licenses/by-nc-nd/4.0/.

ISBN 9798304371599

BS

Publisher BS

Preface

We live in an era of constant connection, where technology permeates every aspect of our lives. Smartphones have become extensions of our bodies, notifications invade our personal space, and the internet offers an endless stream of information. Amidst this digital cacophony, it becomes essential to ask: are we truly living better?

"Unplugged: Digital Minimalism for a Fulfilling Life" invites you to re-evaluate your relationship with technology and rediscover the art of living intentionally. This book is not an anti-technology manifesto but a call to consciousness. It is a practical guide for those seeking to find balance and purpose in their use of digital devices.

Here, we explore strategies to detox your digital life, reduce screen time, and reconnect with the real world. From the importance of moments of silence to the rediscovery of forgotten hobbies, each chapter is a step towards a richer and more meaningful life.

Written with the intent to inspire and empower, this book offers insights, studies, and real-life stories of individuals who have transformed their lives by adopting digital minimalism. With practical guidance and deep reflections, "Unplugged" is an invitation to regain control over your time and attention, and to create a space where technology serves but does not dominate your existence.

May this reading be the beginning of a transformative journey, where you find balance, clarity, and a deeper connection with yourself and the world around you.

Wishing you an enriching experience full of discoveries.

With gratitude,

Contents

Preface	iii
Understanding Digital Minimalism	1
The Case for Intentional Technology Use	5
Quantifying Screen Time	10
Finding Meaning in Analog Alternatives	15
Mastering Digital Decluttering	20
Cultivating Focus and Productivity	24
Building Authentic Relationships	28
Re-evaluating Your Digital Tools	32
Creating a Digital Minimalism Action Plan	37
Overcoming Challenges and Obstacles	42
Navigating Ethical and Sustainable Technology Use	47
Cultivating Mindfulness in a Digital World	52

Personal Growth Through Digital Minimalism 56

Digital Detox: Is It Right for You? 60

Sharing Your Journey with Others 65

The Future of Digital Minimalism 70

Case Studies of Digital Minimalism 74

Conclusion: Reclaiming Your Time and Attention 79

I
Understanding Digital Minimalism

In an era dominated by constant notifications, endless scrolling, and an overwhelming influx of information, the philosophy of digital minimalism emerges as a beacon of clarity—a call to action for a more intentional approach to our digital lives. At its core, digital minimalism is not merely a rejection of technology; rather, it is an invitation to critically assess how and why we engage with the digital tools around us.

Digital minimalism encourages a thoughtful relationship with technology, emphasizing the importance of intentionality in our choices. According to a study published in the *American Journal of Preventive Medicine*, higher levels of screen time are linked to an increase in depression and anxiety, particularly among young adults. This correlation is not merely anecdotal; it underscores the necessity of scrutinizing our digital habits. By choosing technology that aligns with our values and enhances our well-being, we reclaim control over our lives.

Core Principles of Digital Minimalism

Digital minimalism comprises several key principles that can guide individuals in adopting this lifestyle. First and foremost is the **intentional use of technology**. We encourage asking ourselves critical questions: "Does this app or device add significant value to my life?" or "Am I using this tool to serve a purpose, or is it using me?" This conscious filtering fosters a deeper connection with meaningful technology while eliminating distractions.

The second principle is the **reduction of screen time**. Research published in *JAMA Network Open* found that adults who limited their screen time to two hours per day reported significant improvements in overall mental health and productivity. With the average American spending nearly seven hours on screens daily, making a concerted effort to decrease this time can profoundly affect our day-to-day experience and mental state.

Another essential aspect of digital minimalism is **embracing analog alternatives**. A survey by the Pew Research Center found that 93% of adults value in-person interactions over virtual communication for cultivating relationships. Engaging in analog activities like reading physical books or journaling can offer a refreshing break from the digital chaos, enhancing our creativity and deepening our connections.

Benefits of Adopting a Digital Minimalist Lifestyle

The benefits of adopting digital minimalism are extensive and backed by science. Not only does it promote better mental health, but it also fosters improved focus and productivity. A study from Harvard Business Review revealed that employees who minimize digital distractions can boost their productivity by up to 30%. This improved focus allows for deeper work—critical thinking sessions that can spark innovative ideas, ultimately leading to a more fulfilled and satisfying professional life.

Digital minimalism can starkly improve our relationships as well. By prioritizing face-to-face interactions over digital communication, we cultivate richer, more meaningful connections. A report in *The Journal of Social and Personal Relationships* indicated that strong social ties can boost happiness levels, reduce stress, and even promote longevity. It's clear that enhancing our interactions aligns with our innate need for connection.

Common Misconceptions about Minimalism and Technology

Despite the clear advantages of digital minimalism, misconceptions abound. Many equate digital minimalism with a complete withdrawal from technology—a notion that couldn't be further from the truth. In fact, digital minimalism is about integrating technology that enriches our lives while discarding what doesn't serve our goals. A common misunderstanding is that minimalism is synonymous with deprivation; instead, it allows for the curation of experiences and tools that genuinely resonate.

Moreover, some individuals fear that adopting a simplified digital lifestyle may isolate them from the benefits of today's connected world. Yet, studies indicate that intentional use of social media can enhance our experiences, allowing for meaningful connections with communities and shared interests while avoiding the pitfalls of passive consumption.

In conclusion, digital minimalism is a transformative philosophy that empowers us to shape our digital environments. By being intentional about our technology use, we can reclaim our time, improve our mental well-being, enhance our productivity, and foster deeper relationships. As we embark on this journey, let us remember that the goal of digital minimalism is not to eliminate technology but to engage with it in a way that enhances, rather than detracts from, our lives. It's time to take control—your attention, your time, and ultimately, your life are worth it.

II
The Case for Intentional Technology Use

In today's hyper-connected world, technology permeates every aspect of our lives, boasting the ability to enhance our productivity, facilitate communication, and entertain us at the touch of a button. Yet, beneath this glossy facade lies an overwhelming reality: technology often dictates our behaviors and choices instead of the other way around. It's time for a transformational shift toward intentional technology use, a fundamental principle of digital minimalism that can radically improve our daily lives.

The Impact of Technology on Daily Life

Recent studies paint a stark picture of our current technological engagement. According to a study conducted by the Pew Research Center, nearly 50% of adults feel that they are "too dependent" on their smartphones, with 25% reporting constant anxiety when they cannot access their devices. This dependency impacts not only individual well-being but also productivity and interpersonal relationships. Have you ever found yourself absentmindedly scrolling through your social media feed, mindlessly consuming content without any real purpose?

The phenomenon known as "continuous partial attention" — a term coined by Linda Stone, former Microsoft researcher — illustrates our challenge. Stone notes that our attention is divided into countless digital interactions, preventing us from ever fully engaging in any single task or relationship. Furthermore, the American Psychological Association highlights that constant digital engagement is linked to symptoms of anxiety, depression, and burnout. With these clear connections, it becomes imperative to adopt a more intentional approach to technology — one that aligns with our values and priorities instead of eroding them.

Questions to Ask Before Using a Digital Tool

To cultivate a mindset of intentional technology use, start with self-reflection. Here are key questions to consider before reaching for your devices:

1. **What is the purpose of this tool?** — Before using any app or device, assess if it serves a meaningful role in your life. Does it help you connect with loved ones, enhance learning, or contribute to your personal goals?

2. **Am I using this out of necessity or habit?** — Pay attention to your impulses. Is your phone the first thing you reach for during idle moments? Developing awareness around habitual usage can help

identify behaviors that consume your time without providing value.

3. **How does this tool make me feel?** — Reflect on the emotional consequences of your technology use. Does it leave you feeling empowered or drained? Understanding your emotional response helps you evaluate the technology's impact on your well-being.

4. **Are there alternative, more enriching options?** — Consider whether there are analog or offline alternatives that could replace digital habits. Rather than scrolling through social media, how about going for a walk, reading a book, or engaging in a meaningful conversation?

Intentional vs. Unintentional Tech Use

To illustrate the power of intentional technology use, let's examine two contrasting scenarios: intentional versus unintentional tech use.

Intentional Use:

Imagine you set aside a specific hour each evening to engage with educational podcasts related to your field. As you listen, you take notes and reflect on how the information can be implemented in your work. You actively choose to unplug from distractions, immersing yourself entirely in the material. This intentional experience not only enhances your knowledge but also positively impacts your career growth.

Unintentional Use:

Contrast this with spending that same hour mindlessly scrolling through Instagram or aimlessly browsing the web. The content you consume may not resonate with you or contribute to your personal development. You may also find yourself scrolling through endless feeds, only to realize hours have passed without any meaningful engagement. This kind of usage contributes to feelings of unfulfillment and discontent.

The difference in these two scenarios is stark yet revealing. By choosing to engage with technology intentionally, we can reclaim our time and purpose.

The Ethical Imperative

Furthermore, embracing intentional technology use is not only beneficial at the personal level; it carries ethical consequences as well. The tech landscape is filled with companies that leverage persuasive design techniques to keep users hooked. Research from the Stanford Computer Science department has shown that platforms designed for maximum engagement can create a dependency, with algorithms specifically tailored to capture our attention. By becoming digital minimalists and demanding intentionality, we can push back against these maniputive practices, advocating for a healthier relationship with technology.

Conclusion: Reclaiming Control

In a time when our cognitive resources are stretched by constant notifications and distractions, intentional technology use emerges as a vital tool in fulfilling our potential for deeper connections and personal growth. It begins with self-awareness and a commitment to evaluate our digital engagements critically.

Rather than allowing technology to dictate our time and priorities, digital minimalism offers a framework to ensure that we wield technology as a tool for our highest aspirations. So, start asking those pivotal questions, and reclaim your ability to use technology with intention. Embrace the possibilities of a world where your devices serve can only serve you for the better. Dive into the journey of digital minimalism, and take your first step towards reclaiming a more balanced and meaningful life.

III
Quantifying Screen Time

In today's fast-paced digital age, we find ourselves inundated with screens—whether it's our smartphones buzzing with notifications, tablets beckoning with vibrant images, or computers offering endless streams of information. The average person spends over **7 hours a day** engaging with various digital devices, according to a recent report by eMarketer—time that could be better spent on fulfilling activities and relationships. Understanding and quantifying our screen time is not just a matter of curiosity; it is a critical step towards intentional technology use and can profoundly impact our well-being and productivity.

The Importance of Monitoring Screen Time

Monitoring screen time allows individuals to take control of their digital habits, fostering an awareness of how much of their lives are governed by these devices. A study published in the journal **Psychological Science** found a direct correlation between increased screen time and feelings of depression and anxiety. Participants who reported higher levels of screen exposure also exhibited signs of increased loneliness and dissatisfaction in life. The truth is, our screens can often hold us captive, preventing us from engaging in meaningful interactions and activities that enrich our lives.

By regularly tracking screen time, individuals can gain insight into their habits, helping them to identify areas for improvement. A **2021 study by the American Psychological Association** highlights that those who actively monitored their screen time were less likely to experience feelings of burnout and stress compared to those who did not. This data underscores the importance of awareness; by observing our habits, we can begin to make informed choices about how we spend our time.

Tools and Apps for Tracking Digital Usage

Fortunately, the very technology that can consume us also provides tools to help regain our time. Several apps and features are designed specifically for tracking screen use. Here are a few recommendations:

1. **Screen Time (iOS)**: This built-in feature tracks device usage and can even set limits on apps that consume too much time.

2. **Digital Wellbeing (Android)**: Similar to Apple's offering, this tool provides insights into daily usage and allows users to set timers for specific applications.

3. **RescueTime**: A productivity app that runs in the background and tracks time spent on various web-

sites and applications, helping you understand your digital habits in more detail.

4. **Moment**: This app tracks how much you use your phone each day and sends alerts when you exceed your set limits, encouraging better habits.

By regularly utilizing these tools, you not only gather the data needed to make conscious changes but also cultivate a mindset of mindfulness regarding your technology use.

Strategies for Reducing Screen Time Effectively

Once you've started monitoring your screen time and observed your habits, the next step is to implement effective strategies aimed at reducing unnecessary use:

1. **Set Clear Limits**: Establish specific time frames for when you allow yourself to engage with digital devices. For example, you may choose to limit social media to 30 minutes per day.

2. **Prioritize Activities**: Replace digital time with activities that enrich your life. For instance, commit to reading one book a month or exploring a new hobby instead of scrolling through social media.

3. **Technology-Free Zones**: Designate certain areas in your home as technology-free. The bedroom or dining area can become sanctuaries for unplugged interactions and peaceful evenings.

4. **Schedule Downtime**: Carve out specific times in your day dedicated to being screen-free. Use these

slots to connect with family, engage in physical activity, or enjoy quiet reflection.

5. **Mindful Consumption**: Before reaching for your device, ask yourself if it aligns with your personal goals and values. Are you seeking genuine connection, or are you merely filling time? Making mindful choices can drastically reduce mindless scrolling.

The Impact of Reduced Screen Time

Research indicates the benefits of reducing screen time are not just anecdotal but measurable. A study published in the **Journal of Health Psychology** found that individuals who reduced their screen time reported improved sleep quality, increased mood, and enhanced overall life satisfaction. Moreover, individuals observed a surge in in-person interactions and a greater enjoyment of hobbies, contributing to a stronger sense of fulfillment.

In an era where attention is a currency and distractions are plentiful, quantifying and reducing screen time presents a pathway to victory over chaos. You begin to reclaim lost hours and transform them into opportunities for growth, connection, and creativity.

In embracing digital minimalism and implementing these strategies, you are not only fostering a more intentional relationship with technology but also creating space in your life for the things that truly matter. Remember, it's not about the technology itself but how you choose to engage with it. By taking the reins of your digital consumption, you empower yourself to live a more focused, meaningful, and enriched life. The journey towards a healthy digital balance begins with a single step; let it start today.

IV
Finding Meaning in Analog Alternatives

In a world overwhelmingly saturated with digital noise, the allure of analog experiences offers a refreshing refuge. Engaging with analog alternatives is not merely a nostalgic return to the past; it is, in fact, a conscious decision to cultivate deeper connections with our surroundings, ourselves, and each other. The transition from digital reliance to analog engagement can transform not only our routines but also our overall wellbeing. Research overwhelmingly supports this notion, demonstrating that analog practices significantly improve mental health, focus, and interpersonal relationships.

The Benefits of Engaging with Analog Experiences

The psychological benefits of stepping away from screens are monumental. A study published in the journal *Psychological Science* found that individuals who spent time in nature, engaging in physical activities devoid of digital distractions, reported enhanced mood and decreased levels of anxiety. Nature walks, when coupled with analog activities—like sketching in a journal or reading a print book—can yield a remarkable rejuvenation of the spirit.

Further, a study from the University of California, Irvine, revealed that "the mere presence of phone notifications can distract from meaningful tasks." Engaging with analog alternatives, such as writing in a notebook or participating in a board game, not only fosters creativity but also enables individuals to spend uninterrupted time on tasks that hold deeper value. These experiences promote mindfulness and presence, which can easily be diminished in our screen-obsessed lifestyles.

Suggestions for Replacing Digital Habits with Analog Activities

1. **Read a Physical Book**: Instead of scrolling through digital news articles or e-books, pick up a physical book. The tactile engagement and absence of screen light present numerous benefits, including improved comprehension and retention rates. A study from the Norwegian University of Science and Technology found that students who read from physical books exhibited superior focus and cognitive engagement compared to those who read on screens.

2. **Start a Journal**: Writing your thoughts and daily reflections on paper encourages mindfulness and greater self-awareness. Journaling has been shown to reduce stress and improve mental clarity. A study published in the *Journal of Experimental Psychology* indicated that expressive writing can en-

hance emotional intelligence and facilitate emotional healing.

3. **Engage in Board Games or Puzzles**: Spend quality time with family and friends by playing board games or solving puzzles together. Research by the *American Psychological Association* suggests that shared activities, especially face-to-face interactions, significantly strengthen interpersonal bonds and enhance communication skills.

4. **Explore Outdoor Activities**: Instead of binge-watching shows or scrolling through social media, consider pursuing outdoor activities—hiking, biking, or simply walking. A study from the University of Michigan found that spending time in green spaces significantly boosts cognitive functioning and boosts creativity.

5. **Practice Crafting or Art**: Engage in crafts, painting, or drawing. Not only does art provide a creative outlet, but studies show that engaging in artistic activities can elevate mood and reduce stress. A report from the *American Journal of Public Health* highlights that artistic engagement can serve as a powerful therapeutic tool, fostering personal growth and emotional stability.

Case Studies of Successful Transitions to Analog Methods

Numerous success stories illustrate the benefits of transitioning to analog methods. Consider the case of a graphic designer who, initially overwhelmed by digital distractions, made the shift from digital sketching to using pencil and paper. Within weeks, she reported feeling more inspired and focused, producing higher-quality work with greater creativity—an outcome supported by research from the *Journal of Design History* which links tactile engagement in the design process to increased innovation.

Another inspiring example is that of a family who decided to unfollow all digital entertainment sources for a summer in favor of analog experiences. They replaced screen time with reading sessions, outdoor adventures, and game nights. At the end of the summer, not only did they report strengthened family relationships, but they also noted a marked improvement in individual happiness levels—data that resonates with findings from the *Journal of Happiness Studies* that emphasize relational bonding and happiness among families engaging in analog activities together.

Conclusion

Embracing analog alternatives does more than simply fill our time; it enriches our experiences, nurtures our relationships, and promotes a healthier mindset. With mounting scientific evidence demonstrating the benefits of reduced screen time and increased engagement in analog activities, it becomes increasingly clear that opting for the tangible over the digital can significantly elevate the quality of our lives.

As we find meaning in analog experiences, we reclaim our attention, foster connections, and cultivate a deeper appreciation for the world around us. Are we ready to rediscover the profound joy of simple pleasures? The journey begins with a single, intentional choice to step away from the screen and into our vibrant, multi-dimensional lives.

V
Mastering Digital Decluttering

In a world overwhelmed by information, the concept of digital decluttering has emerged as a beacon of clarity and focus. Just as physical clutter can weigh us down and inhibit our productivity, digital clutter has similarly detrimental effects on our mental well-being and efficiency. Decluttering our digital spaces is not merely a task—it's a transformative practice. Research indicates that digital clutter can lead to cognitive overload, with studies revealing that multitasking and the presence of distractions can decrease productivity by as much as 40% (Mark, Gudith, & Klocke, 2008). Thus, mastering digital decluttering is imperative for those seeking to embrace a digital minimalist lifestyle.

Steps to Declutter Digital Spaces

1. **Start with Intentionality**: Before diving into the decluttering process, reflect on your values and goals. Ask yourself questions like: Which digital tools and platforms genuinely enhance my life? Which ones merely serve as distractions? Aligning

your decluttering efforts with your personal objectives will guide your decisions, enabling you to remove the excess and focus on what brings value.

2. **Tackle One Area at a Time**: Digital clutter can manifest in various forms—emails, files, apps, and social media accounts. Commit to decluttering one area at a time to avoid feeling overwhelmed. For example, dedicate a specific session to organizing your email inbox. The average office worker spends 28% of their workweek managing emails (McKinsey Global Institute, 2012). Therefore, a clean inbox can dramatically improve your efficiency.

3. **Implement the 'Four Ds'**: When sorting through your digital content, employ the 'Four Ds'—Delete, Delegate, Defer, and Do. If something no longer serves a purpose, delete it. If it requires action but isn't your responsibility, delegate it. If it can wait, defer it. Finally, for items demanding immediate attention, just do it. This methodological approach can simplify decision-making and accelerate the decluttering process.

4. **Organize and Archive**: After identifying what to keep, organize your files into clear, categorized folders. Use consistent naming conventions and avoid cryptic files. Studies show that maintaining an organized digital environment can improve focus and reduce anxiety levels (Zhang et al., 2020). Additionally, regularly archiving old documents keeps your workspace uncluttered and manageable.

5. **Unsubscribe and Unfollow**: Social media and online subscriptions can pile up, extracting precious mental energy. Consider the impact of what you consume daily. Launched in 2019, the "Unsubscribe Challenge" encouraged participants to unsubscribe from emails that added no value. Reactions showed that participants experienced a newfound clarity and reduced feelings of being overwhelmed. Unfollowing accounts that bring negativity or serve no purpose can foster a healthier digital environment, improving your overall well-being.

Tips for Organizing Emails, Files, and Apps

- **Email Tags and Folders**: Use tags and folders to categorize emails by projects, urgency, or clients. Email platforms like Gmail allow you to create labels, ensuring critical messages are easily accessible without the clutter.

- **Cloud Storage Solutions**: Platforms such as Google Drive, Dropbox, or OneDrive offer sustainable solutions for organizing and accessing files from anywhere. Create a habit of regularly reviewing and deleting outdated files from these cloud services.

- **Home Screen Optimization**: Your smartphone is a gateway to digital overload. Consider removing apps that you rarely use and consolidating your most-used apps into easily accessible folders. A study by the Pew Research Center (2018) suggested that simplifying our device interfaces can promote better focus and engagement.

Creating a Sustainable Decluttering Routine

Decluttering should not be a one-time event but rather an ongoing process. Establish a regular schedule—weekly or monthly—to review your digital spaces. Implement the '10-Minute Rule'—set a timer for ten minutes, during which you focus solely on decluttering one digital space. This approach fosters consistency, making decluttering less daunting and more integrated into your lifestyle.

Additionally, create a habit of evaluating new digital tools before incorporating them. Ask yourself whether these tools serve a specific purpose aligned with your goals. Research indicates that practicing intentionality in technology use can result in profound productivity gains (Koh, 2023).

Conclusion

Mastering digital decluttering is an essential step toward embracing the principles of digital minimalism. The psychological benefits of a streamlined digital space—reduced anxiety, increased focus, and improved productivity—cannot be overstated. In a landscape dominated by distractions, the act of decluttering empowers you to reclaim your attention and time. As you embark on this journey, remember that each small step paves the way for a more intentional and fulfilling digital existence. With your newly organized digital space, you can focus on what truly matters, paving the way for personal growth and meaningful connections. Ultimately, digital decluttering is the first powerful stride on your path to mastering a minimalist digital life.

VI
Cultivating Focus and Productivity

In a world where notifications chime at every turn and digital distractions lurk in every corner of our screens, cultivating focus and productivity may seem like an elusive goal. Yet, recent studies reveal that attention is a finite resource, and how we manage it can significantly impact our performance and overall well-being. A shift towards digital minimalism can empower individuals to reclaim their focus, enhance productivity, and ultimately lead a more fulfilling life.

Identifying Digital Distractions

Start by recognizing the digital distractions that infiltrate your daily routine. Research indicates that the average person checks their phone every 12 minutes, equating to over 80 times a day (TechJury, 2023). Each notification, whether from social media, email, or messaging platforms, pulls your attention away from the task at hand, often leading to diminished productivity.

Furthermore, a study by the University of California, Irvine, found that it takes an average of 23 minutes to regain focus after an interruption (Mark et al., 2008). This highlights the profound impact that digital distractions can have on our productivity levels. Understanding these distractions is the first step in overcoming them.

Techniques for Enhancing Concentration

To counteract the forces of distraction, several techniques can be implemented to foster a deeper focus in our work and daily lives. Here are some practical strategies based on scientific research and expert recommendations:

1. **The Pomodoro Technique**: This time management method involves working in concentrated bursts followed by short breaks. A study by the University of Illinois found that short breaks can enhance focus and sustain attention, preventing mental fatigue (Ariga & Lleras, 2011). By dividing your tasks into 25-minute segments, followed by a five-minute break, you not only boost your concentration but also optimize your productivity.

2. **Digital Detox Zones**: Create specific areas or times in your day where technology is off-limits. Research shows that environments free from screen interruptions can enhance cognitive performance. A study conducted by the University of Kent demonstrated that participants working in more traditional, low-tech environments produced better quality work and had higher focus than those in more digitally infused settings (Hale, 2016).

3. **Mindfulness Practices**: Introducing mindfulness into your daily routine can significantly enhance focus and reduce stress. According to a study in the journal Psychological Science, participants who underwent mindfulness training exhibited improved attention and cognitive flexibility (Zeidan et al., 2010). Simple practices like meditation or mindful breathing can also help cultivate a mental state geared towards sustained concentration.

The Importance of Deep Work

In the age of constant connectivity, the concept of "deep work"—a term popularized by Cal Newport—has never been more relevant. Deep work refers to the ability to focus without distraction on cognitively demanding tasks. According to Newport, cultivating this skill not only boosts productivity but also allows you to produce better quality work and achieve greater satisfaction from your achievements.

A survey of over 1,000 knowledge workers by the productivity software company Atlassian found that most employees report spending only about a third of their workweek on actual productive work, with distractions cutting into valuable time (Atlassian, 2019). By adopting the principles of digital minimalism, you can prioritize deep work and minimize these treacherous distractions, leading to more meaningful outputs.

Regular Breaks and Recovery

While pushing to complete tasks can be tempting, research shows that taking regular breaks is critical for maintaining high levels of productivity (Leroy, 2009).

Incorporating short breaks after periods of intense focus can recharge your brain, allowing for improved retention and creativity. Establishing a system that includes strategic breaks—such as a short walk, stretching, or even engaging in an analog hobby—can invigorate your mind and enhance your productivity.

Conclusion

Mindfully navigating the digital landscape can transform chaotic distractions into focused productivity. By understanding the effects of digital distractions, implementing techniques such as the Pomodoro Technique, establishing digital detox zones, and prioritizing mindfulness and deep work, you can take significant strides towards a more productive life.

Digital minimalism provides a pathway to cultivating focus and enhancing your productivity, enabling you to reclaim your time and direct your efforts toward what truly matters. Start today—reduce the noise, sharpen your focus, and watch as your productivity flourishes in an age of distraction.

VII
Building Authentic Relationships

In an age dominated by digital communication, it is all too easy to overlook the profound importance of face-to-face interaction. We might be an Instagram follower or a Facebook friend, but these connections often lack the depth and authenticity of in-person relationships. The philosophy of digital minimalism advocates for a recalibration of our interactions, urging us to prioritize genuine, meaningful connections over superficial online engagements.

The Importance of In-Person Interactions

Research has consistently shown that in-person interactions are vital for emotional and psychological well-being. A study conducted by the Harvard Study of Adult Development, one of the longest-running studies of adult life, found that social connections are a fundamental predictor of happiness. Notably, individuals who reported feeling supported and connected to others had better health outcomes, demonstrating that quality relationships not only enhance emotional well-being but also improve physical health.

Conversely, excessive reliance on digital communication has been linked to feelings of loneliness and depression. A survey published in the American Journal of Preventive Medicine highlighted that increased social media use is associated with increased feelings of isolation. The irony is striking: the very platforms designed to connect us often leave us feeling more disconnected.

Fostering Connections Without Screens

To build authentic relationships, we must confront the ways technology has reshaped our social habits. Here are some practical strategies to help cultivate deeper connections without the interference of screens:

1. **Organize Technology-Free Gatherings**: Host events where attendees are encouraged to leave their devices behind. This can take the form of potlucks, game nights, or outdoor activities. The absence of screens can provoke spontaneous conversations and shared experiences that deeply bond people.

2. **Engage in Shared Activities**: Whether it's taking a cooking class, hiking, or participating in community service, shared activities create opportunities for genuine connection and collaboration. According to Dr. Barbara Fredrickson's research on positive emotions, shared experiences contribute to building stronger relationships by eliciting feelings of joy and connection.

3. **Practice Active Listening**: In an era of constant distractions, truly listening has become a rare skill. Make a conscious effort to engage in conversations with full attention. Studies have shown that individuals who practice active listening are more likely to build trust and rapport with others, fostering meaningful relationships.

4. **Schedule Regular Face-to-Face Interactions**: Make it a habit to schedule time with family and friends, whether it's a weekly dinner or a monthly outing. The mere act of putting these interactions on your calendar can significantly enhance your commitment to nurturing relationships.

The Benefits of Technology-Free Gatherings

The impact of technology-free interactions extends beyond mere connection; it fosters emotional enrichment and community engagement. A University of Virginia study found that people engaged in fake social media interactions report feeling lonelier than those who opt for direct, in-person conversations. The sense of belonging and community that comes from these face-to-face experiences can reduce anxiety and boost happiness levels.

Moreover, technology-free gatherings encourage vulnerability, an essential ingredient for deep connections. When phones are switched off, individuals feel freer to express their emotions and thoughts candidly. Brené Brown, the renowned researcher on vulnerability, states, "Vulnerability is the birthplace of innovation, creativity, and change." By embracing vulnerability in our relationships, we open pathways to richer, more meaningful interactions.

In addition, fostering a tech-free environment influences the dynamics of group interactions positively. A study in the journal *Environment and Behavior* indicated that participants who engaged in discussions without the presence of technology produced more cooperative and cohesive group dynamics.

Conclusion

Digital minimalism advocates for a return to the roots of human connection. By recognizing the profound effects of genuine interactions and prioritizing them in our lives, we can mitigate the digital distractions that often dilute the quality of our relationships. Investing time and energy in building authentic connections not only enhances our personal relationships but also cultivates a more fulfilling and purposeful life.

Embrace the challenge of stepping away from screens and immersing yourself in the richness of human connection. Commit to this practice, and watch as your relationships blossom in unexpected and rewarding ways. Rediscover the joy of shared laughter, rich conversations, and the simple presence of those who matter most—because ultimately, it is these relationships that define our happiness and well-being in this digital age.

VIII
Re-evaluating Your Digital Tools

In an age where technology permeates nearly every aspect of our lives, a critical question emerges: Are the digital tools at our disposal genuinely serving our needs and aligning with our values? As we delve into the realm of digital minimalism, re-evaluating the technology we choose to engage with becomes essential. A deliberate inventory of our digital tools can lead to profound transformations, enhancing our well-being, focus, and fulfillment.

Conducting a Personal Inventory of Technology Use

To begin this journey of reassessment, we must first conduct a personal inventory of the technology currently in our lives. Research indicates that individuals significantly underestimate the time spent on digital devices—one study found that participants believed they spent an average of only one hour less on their devices than they actually did. In reality, the average individual spends over seven hours per day on screens, a figure that can be alarming when you consider the lost opportunities for personal interactions and passions (Pew Research Center).

Start by documenting each digital tool—apps, social media platforms, websites, and devices—that you routinely use. Once enumerated, ask yourself:

- **Purpose**: What is the primary purpose of this tool?
- **Value**: Does it genuinely contribute to my life goals and values?
- **Impact**: How does it affect my mood, relationships, and overall well-being?

This contemplation can be eye-opening. For example, a widely used social media app may provide entertainment and a sense of connection; however, it may also invoke feelings of inadequacy, anxiety, or envy—emotions that detract from well-being. Recognizing the negative impacts of certain tools empowers individuals to make informed choices.

Tools That Align with Goals and Values

Adopting a digital minimalist mindset means leaning into technology that serves your most vital objectives. Studies have shown that aligning daily actions with personal values leads to higher satisfaction and fulfillment. For example, prioritizing communication tools that foster genuine connections over those that promote superficial interactions can significantly enhance the quality of your relationships (Smith & Duggan, 2013).

Consider the most salient aspects of your life—career, relationships, health, and personal growth—and evaluate whether your existing tools contribute positively in these domains. Are you using productivity apps to streamline your work process, or are they merely a distraction, causing task-switching that diminishes focus? Research indicates that multitasking can reduce productivity by as much as 40%, emphasizing the need to reflect on the efficiency of our tools (American Psychological Association).

Making Informed Decisions About Technology Investments

Once you have assessed your digital tools and sorted them into valuable and non-essential categories, the next step is to make informed decisions about which tools to keep and which to part with. This process often feels daunting, particularly in a tech-centric culture that values constant connectivity. However, remember that it is not about rejecting technology outright; it's about making educated choices that enhance your lifestyle.

Focus on areas where you can reallocate your time and energy. For instance, if you find that a particular app creates more stress than joy, explore alternatives that align better with your intentions. A study from the Journal of Computer-Mediated Communication highlighted that phone applications with features designed to enhance well-being (like mindfulness or wellness tracking) can remain an integral part of your tech ecosystem, while apps that induce anxiety or compel compulsive checking can be deleted.

The Long-Term Benefits of a Purposeful Tech Landscape

Re-evaluating your digital tools can lead to significant long-term benefits. By curating a technology environment that resonates with your goals and values, you create space for personal growth, deeper relationships, and improved overall satisfaction. Research from the University of California, Irvine, shows that minimizing distractions in the digital workspace leads not only to greater focus but also enhances creativity and innovation.

Moreover, adopting this method of mindful evaluation acts as a catalyst for other practices embraced within digital minimalism, such as digital decluttering and upping engagement in analog alternatives. As you streamline your digital landscape, you will find that less truly is more; this fundamental shift encourages you to invest more time and energy in endeavors that forge a stronger connection to your authentic self and experiences.

Conclusion: Empowering Your Digital Journey

The act of re-evaluating your digital tools is a powerful step towards a more intentional, meaningful life. By consciously selecting technologies that align with your core values and objectives, you reclaim time and mental space that might have been previously consumed by unnecessary distractions. This process doesn't just enrich your relationship with technology—it paves the way for enhanced fulfillment and personal growth in the broader narrative of your life.

As you embark on this path of digital assessment, remember that every decision you make has the potential to significantly elevate your quality of life. Embrace this opportunity to shape a technology landscape that not only fulfills your immediate needs but also echoes your long-term aspirations. Your journey toward digital minimalism starts with the courage to re-evaluate your tools—make it count!

IX
Creating a Digital Minimalism Action Plan

In an era swamped with notifications, endless scrolling, and relentless digital distractions, the notion of digital minimalism can feel not just necessary, but revolutionary. Yet, understanding the philosophy is one thing; implementing it is another. Now is the time to take control. Imagine a life where technology serves your goals rather than dictates your behavior. This chapter will guide you in creating a personalized Digital Minimalism Action Plan, complete with practical steps, timelines, and accountability measures designed to usher you into a more intentional relationship with technology.

Step 1: Self-Assessment—Understanding Your Current Relationship with Technology

The journey toward digital minimalism begins with self-reflection. Start by assessing your current technology usage. Spend one week meticulously tracking your screen time, using apps like RescueTime or Screen Time for iOS. You might be surprised to learn that, according to a study by Nielsen, the average American spends over 11 hours per day interacting with media. Imagine reclaiming just a fraction of that time!

Once you have a clear picture, reflect on the following questions:

- Which digital tools do you use most frequently?

- Do these tools support your personal goals and values?

- When do you feel happiest or most engaged while using technology?

These questions will help pinpoint where adjustments are needed.

Step 2: Set Clear and Realistic Objectives

With insights from your self-assessment, it's time to establish specific objectives. Research from the American Psychological Association indicates that goal-setting increases the likelihood of achieving personal growth outcomes. Here's how you can frame your objectives using the SMART criteria (Specific, Measurable, Achievable, Relevant, Time-bound):

1. **Specific**: Rather than a vague goal like "reduce screen time," specify: "Decrease my social media use to 30 minutes a day."

2. **Measurable**: Incorporate metrics: "Monitor my usage with the screen time app weekly."

3. **Achievable**: Ensure your goals are realistic. For instance, cutting down from 5 hours of gaming to 1 hour might be ambitious for some.

4. **Relevant**: Align your objectives with your core values. If relationships matter most, prioritize face-to-face interactions.

5. **Time-bound**: Establish a timeline. Aim to meet your goal within one month.

Step 3: Develop Actionable Strategies

Now that you have objectives set, outline specific steps to achieve them. If your goal is to reduce social media use, consider these actionable strategies:

- **Schedule Tech-Free Time**: Allocate specific hours in your day or week for no digital distractions. Research from the University of California indicates that it may take up to 23 minutes to regain focus after a digital interruption; safeguarding uninterrupted time becomes crucial for productivity.

- **Replace with Analog Alternatives**: Seek analog activities as substitutes for digital habits. If you often find yourself scrolling during coffee breaks, replace that time with a physical book or journaling—activities shown to enhance cognitive processing and emotional well-being.

- **Create a Digital Diet**: Just as one would moderate food intake, adopt a "digital diet." Reduce the number of apps on your phone by uninstalling those that don't add value. A study published in the International Journal of Human-Computer Interaction shows that fewer apps correlate with lower anxiety levels and better focus.

Step 4: Accountability and Support

Creating an action plan does not mean walking this path alone. Find a buddy or community to share your journey with, amplifying your commitment. Research from the Journal of Consulting and Clinical Psychology shows that social support increases the likelihood of achieving goals. Utilize social media—not as a distraction, but as a tool for accountability. Share your goals with friends or join an online group committed to digital minimalism.

Step 5: Schedule Regular Check-ins

Your digital minimalism journey is ongoing. Schedule weekly or bi-weekly check-ins with yourself to evaluate your progress. Reflect on the changes you've made:

- Are you spending less time engulfed in screens?
- Have you identified additional tools or habits that are not beneficial?

These reflections will help you course-correct as needed, ensuring the plan continues to evolve.

Step 6: Emphasize Flexibility and Mindfulness

Finally, imbue your action plan with flexibility and mindfulness. Rigid plans can lead to frustration, particularly when life throws curveballs. Incorporate periods of mindfulness into your routine, whether through meditation, yoga, or simply a moment to breathe. Research published in the journal Psychological Science finds that mindfulness can improve focus and emotional regulation, enhancing your relationship with technology.

Conclusion

Creating a Digital Minimalism Action Plan empowers you to reclaim your time, attention, and life. The decision to curate your digital environment intentionally can lead to profound benefits in mental health, relationships, and personal fulfillment. By implementing a plan tailored specifically to your goals and context, you're not just adopting minimalism; you're embarking on a journey toward a more meaningful, focused existence. Begin today, step into the future armed with clarity and purpose, and watch as the noise of digital distractions fades away, making space for what truly matters.

X
Overcoming Challenges and Obstacles

Embracing digital minimalism can feel like stepping into uncharted territory, marked by a desire for clarity and balance. Yet, as with any significant lifestyle change, the road ahead is often obstructed by challenges that threaten to derail our best intentions. Understanding these obstacles—and employing effective strategies to overcome them—can empower you to stay committed to a more intentional relationship with technology. The stakes are higher than mere inconvenience; they affect not only our productivity but also our well-being and sense of fulfillment.

Recognizing Common Pitfalls

The first step in overcoming challenges is recognizing what lies in your path. Common pitfalls in the journey to digital minimalism include:

1. **Resistance to Change:** Change is hard, especially when it feels like our social lives, work, and even our entertainment are intertwined with technology. Research shows that the human brain is wired to resist change; we often prefer the familiarity of the status quo (Prochaska & DiClemente, 1983). Consequently, the comfort of existing digital habits can be a formidable force.

2. **Fear of Missing Out (FOMO):** The pervasive culture of "always being connected" can induce anxiety around missing something important. A 2018 study found that individuals who experience high levels of FOMO are more likely to engage in social media, which, paradoxically, can exacerbate feelings of loneliness and dissatisfaction (Hunt et al., 2018).

3. **Social Pressure:** Friends and family may not understand your commitment to digital minimalism. The fear of social isolation can deter you from embarking on this journey. According to a survey by Pew Research, around 68% of adults report feeling pressure to stay connected online (Perrin & Duggan, 2015).

4. **Information Overload:** The digital space is inundated with tips and strategies for minimalism, leading to confusion and overwhelm. A report from the National Center for Biotechnology Information found that excessive choices can lead to decision paralysis, making it harder to act (Schwartz, 2004).

Strategies for Overcoming Resistance

Once you recognize these challenges, you can implement strategies to overcome them. Here are some targeted approaches backed by scientific insights:

1. **Start Small:** The path to digital minimalism doesn't require an all-or-nothing approach. Begin with small, manageable changes that align with your goals. Research in behavior modification suggests that incremental changes are more sustainable (Hollon et al., 2002). Commit to reducing your screen time by just 10% in the first week, then gradually increase this as you become more comfortable.

2. **Create a Support Network:** Leverage the power of community. Forming or joining a support group can provide reassurance and motivation as you navigate your digital minimalism journey. According to a study by Wymer et al. (2008), social support is a critical factor for maintaining behavior change. Sharing your challenges and triumphs with others can reinforce your commitment.

3. **Practice Mindfulness:** Cultivating mindfulness can serve as an essential tool for managing FOMO and social pressure. Techniques such as meditation and deep breathing help ground you in the present moment, minimizing anxiety about disconnection. Research highlights that mindfulness practices can significantly reduce stress and improve emotional regulation (Kabat-Zinn, 2003).

4. **Set Boundaries:** Establish clear boundaries between technology and personal time. This might

involve designating tech-free zones in your home or scheduling specific hours for engaging with digital devices. A study by Rosen et al. (2013) found that creating structured tech boundaries leads to improved focus and overall satisfaction.

5. **Reflect Regularly:** Make time to reflect on your digital habits and the benefits of minimalism you've experienced. Journaling or self-assessment can clarify your progress and reinforce your motivations. Research suggests that reflection enhances commitment to behavioral changes (Gollwitzer et al., 1990).

The Power of Long-Term Commitment

While challenges are an inevitable part of the journey, succumbing to them is not the end game. A 2019 study revealed that the perceived benefits of reduced digital engagement—a greater sense of fulfillment, mindfulness, and authentic relationships—far outweigh the initial discomfort of change (Amichai-Hamburger et al., 2019).

It is crucial not to judge your progress too harshly or give up when setbacks occur. Just as developing any skill takes time and perseverance, so too does fostering a lifestyle of digital minimalism. Even small victories deserve recognition, as they cumulatively lead to significant transformations.

Encouragement for Your Journey

As you navigate the complexities of digital minimalism, remember this is a journey you are choosing for yourself. The drive towards intentionality will yield lasting benefits in your life—enhanced focus, deeper relationships, and ultimately, a more fulfilling existence. Each step you take towards overcoming obstacles only strengthens your resolve and furthers your commitment to live intentionally in an increasingly distracted world.

In summary, embrace the challenges of digital minimalism as valuable teachers. Understand what stands in your way, employ strategies to mitigate those obstacles, and remember: the pursuit of a more intentional and impactful digital life is not just romantic idealism; it is a science-backed pathway to greater well-being. The choice to minimize the digital noise and focus on what truly matters is, ultimately, a power that lies within you.

XI
Navigating Ethical and Sustainable Technology Use

In our modern, technology-driven society, it's crucial to consider not just how we use technology, but also how it's made and what impact it has on the world around us. As digital minimalists, adopting a mindset of ethical and sustainable technology use is integral to the philosophy. It's not merely about reducing screen time or decluttering your digital life; it's about making informed decisions that align with our values and contribute positively to society and the environment.

Understanding the Environmental Effects of Tech Consumption

Every time we upgrade our devices or purchase new gadgets, we contribute to a significant environmental footprint. According to a report by the Global e-Sustainability Initiative (GeSI), information and communications technology (ICT) is responsible for approximately 4% of global greenhouse gas emissions—

equivalent to that of the aviation industry. This number could grow as demand for technology increases, highlighting the urgency for more sustainable practices.

The life cycle of electronic devices—from extraction of raw materials to manufacturing, distribution, use, and disposal—poses substantial environmental challenges. For instance, the extraction of metals like cobalt and lithium can result in deforestation, loss of biodiversity, and significant water usage. Furthermore, many electronic devices consist of non-biodegradable materials, leading to landfill overflow and hazardous waste pollution. By being mindful of our consumption, we can lessen our environmental impact and foster a healthier planet for future generations.

Making Informed Choices about Device Purchases and Upgrades

Navigating the tech marketplace can often feel overwhelming, characterized by marketing strategies enticing consumers to constantly upgrade. However, embracing digital minimalism means assessing whether a new device truly adds value to your life. In fact, a 2022 study published in the Journal of Cleaner Production found that extending the lifespan of electronics by just one year could reduce carbon emissions by up to 75% per unit.

Before making a purchase, ask yourself:

- **Do I need this device?** Evaluate whether the new technology will genuinely enhance your productivity or well-being.

- **How long do I plan to use it?** Understanding your long-term needs can help prevent unnecessary upgrades.

- **What's the company's track record?** Research the brand's commitment to sustainability, such as responsible sourcing, fair labor practices, and recycling initiatives.

By scrutinizing the companies we support, we can prioritize those that share our ethical values. Brands like Fairphone, which focuses on sustainable sourcing and fair labor conditions, embody this philosophy and are redefining what responsible tech looks like.

Supporting Companies with Ethical Practices

Supporting companies that operate ethically not only aligns with your personal values but also exerts pressure on other organizations to adopt sustainable practices. The tech industry is known for its opacity regarding supply chains and labor practices. A study from the Business & Human Rights Resource Centre revealed that over 70% of the largest technology firms failed to meet basic standards of transparency in their supply chains, leaving ample room for exploitation and environmental degradation.

Before making a purchase, consider:

- **What are the company's sustainability commitments?** Investigate if they have pledges for carbon neutrality, waste reduction, or ethical labor standards.

- **How do they handle e-waste?** Inquire whether a company has a take-back program to ensure responsible recycling of old devices.

- **Are they involved in social initiatives?** Evaluate if the company invests in local communities or supports educational programs, promoting a better society.

By choosing to support businesses that align with these principles, we consciously contribute to a market that values sustainability, fairness, and ethical practices.

Conclusion: The Power of Thoughtful Technology Use

Adopting a digital minimalist approach extends beyond personal convenience. It reflects a conscious commitment to ethical and sustainable technology use in our interconnected world. By recognizing the impact of our consumption and making intentional choices, we can contribute to a more sustainable future.

Let this understanding guide your decisions. Advocating for ethical practices and sustainable technology not only enhances your own life but also promotes a healthier environment and society. Together, we can leverage the power of technology to create positive change while remaining true to the principles of digital minimalism. Embrace the philosophy—be intentional with your technology use, scrutinize your purchases, and promote ethical standards. The positive repercussions are profound, affecting not only our individual lives but also the broader global context. As digital minimalists, let us be champions for a future that upholds our values and respects our planet.

XII
Cultivating Mindfulness in a Digital World

In a society increasingly dominated by screens and digital interfaces, the ability to cultivate mindfulness is not just a skill but an essential lifeline. The practice of mindfulness, defined as the ability to be fully present in the moment, significantly enriches our lives, especially when it comes to our relationship with technology. In this chapter, we will explore the integral role mindfulness plays in the philosophy of digital minimalism, its benefits, and practical techniques to integrate mindfulness into our digital interactions.

Understanding Mindfulness in the Digital Context

Mindfulness helps us enhance our awareness of the present, providing clarity and insight amid the barrage of notifications and distractions. A study published in the journal *Psychological Science* highlights that mindfulness practices can increase our awareness of how technology impacts our mental health (Zeidan et al., 2010). By regularly engaging in mindfulness practices, individuals can disrupt habitual, unintentional technology use and replace it with conscious, purposeful engagement. This transformation can significantly mitigate the mental noise associated with excessive digital consumption, effectively enhancing our quality of life.

Techniques for Integrating Mindfulness into Technology Use

1. **Mindful Check-Ins**: Start each day with a simple exercise: before reaching for your phone, take a moment to breathe deeply and express gratitude for the technology that supports your goals. Practicing this before any digital engagement helps reset your intention and can significantly alter how you interact with technology throughout the day.

2. **Set Boundaries**: Create specific times during your day that are tech-free zones. Research from the University of California, Irvine, found that being continually available through digital devices leads to mental fatigue and stress (Mark et al., 2014). Establishing boundaries fosters the ability to focus on the present moment by freeing your mind from the incessant lure of notifications and interruptions.

3. **Single-Tasking**: In our hyper-connected world, multitasking may seem like the norm, but studies show that it reduces productivity and increases cognitive overload (Rubinstein et al., 2001). Instead, practice single-tasking by dedicating undivided attention to one task at a time. Whether re-

sponding to emails or reading an article, immerse yourself fully in the task. This not only improves efficiency but also enhances the quality of your output.

4. **Digital Detox Breaks**: Allocate time during your day for intentional breaks away from screens. Engage in activities that promote connection with your surroundings, such as taking a walk outdoors or engaging in conversation with a friend. A study by the University of Michigan found that spending time in natural environments significantly boosts cognitive function and well-being (Berman et al., 2012).

5. **Reflective Journaling**: Take time to reflect on your digital experiences through journaling. Write about your interactions with technology—how they made you feel, what you enjoyed, and what felt overwhelming. This regular practice can help you identify patterns in your technology use and refine it to better align with your values and intentions.

Benefits of a Mindful Approach to Digital Interactions

The benefits of integrating mindfulness into our digital lives are profound. Research indicates that mindfulness can lead to decreased stress levels, improved emotional regulation, and enhanced overall well-being (Keng et al., 2011). Furthermore, by practicing mindfulness, we can cultivate a greater sense of presence in our interactions, whether with friends or coworkers, ultimately enhancing the quality of our relationships.

Additionally, mindfulness can alleviate feelings of anxiety often associated with social media use. Rather than mindlessly scrolling through feeds, practicing mindfulness encourages users to engage in more meaningful interactions. Studies suggest that mindful social media use correlates with feelings of greater happiness and satisfaction (Valkenburg & Peter, 2007).

The Path Forward

Incorporating mindfulness into our digital lives is not merely a trend; it is a necessary evolution towards a more fulfilling existence. As we simplify our digital interactions and become more intentional in our technology use, we liberate ourselves from the compulsion to constantly seek validation and engagement from external sources.

As you reflect on your relationship with technology, consider how mindfulness can serve as your guide. By being present in the moment and intentionally choosing when and how to engage with technology, you reclaim control over your digital narrative.

In a world that spins faster with each technological advancement, mindful engagement offers a sanctuary. It encourages us to breathe, to pause, and to appreciate the power of the present moment—not just as passive consumers of technology, but as intentional stewards of our digital lives. Embrace mindfulness, and watch as it transforms your relationship with technology into a tool that truly enriches your life, aligning seamlessly with your values and aspirations.

XIII
Personal Growth Through Digital Minimalism

In a world brimming with digital distractions, finding clarity and focus can often seem like an insurmountable challenge. Yet, embracing digital minimalism presents an unparalleled opportunity for personal growth. By intentionally reducing digital noise, we clear the path for meaningful development in various aspects of our lives. Numerous studies have shown a direct correlation between decreased screen time and enhanced physical and mental well-being, leading to better decision-making, heightened creativity, and a deeper sense of fulfillment.

The Science Behind Digital Minimalism and Personal Growth

A compelling study published in the journal *Psychological Science* found that individuals who limit their screen time report higher levels of happiness and life satisfaction. In a survey of over 2,500 participants, researchers discovered that those who engaged less with social media experienced a significant reduction in feelings of anxiety and depression. This link between reduced digital engagement and emotional well-being is a powerful testament to how digital minimalism can foster personal growth.

Moreover, when we practice intentional technology use, our cognitive abilities improve. Research conducted by the American Psychological Association reveals that multitasking with digital devices—often seen as a skill in our increasingly tech-driven society—actually diminishes focus and productivity. By minimizing digital distractions, individuals can engage in deep work, a state that promotes creativity and innovation, allowing personal goals and priorities to flourish.

Setting Personal Goals and Priorities

Digital minimalism encourages us to reassess how we allocate our time and energy. It encourages not just the questioning of what technology we use, but also why we use it. By identifying our core values and aligning our digital activities with these values, we lay the groundwork for meaningful personal development.

To illustrate this, consider the practice of goal-setting within a digital minimalist framework. Instead of succumbing to the compulsive pull of digital notifications and incessant online updates, digital minimalists engage in a proactive approach to goal-setting. For instance, utilizing techniques such as SMART (Specific, Measurable, Achievable, Relevant, Time-bound) goals allows individuals to define their objectives clearly. When distractions are minimized, the focus shifts from merely reacting to life's chaos to actively pursuing well-defined aspirations.

Real-Life Examples of Growth Through Minimalism

Several influential figures have shared how embracing digital minimalism has led to transformative personal growth. Cal Newport, author of *Deep Work*, advocates for the importance of focused work over shallow distractions. He demonstrates through various case studies how academia, creative fields, and corporate settings benefit immensely from minimal digital interference. Newport himself has found that by structuring his time away from screens, he has published several influential works and developed insightful ideas that challenge conventional wisdom regarding the intersection of technology and productivity.

Another example is the story of a successful entrepreneur, who decided to limit her screen time to foster creativity and connection within her team. By removing the constant influx of emails and messages, she freed up time to engage in face-to-face discussions and creative brainstorming sessions. This resulted in not only improved relationships within her team but also innovative solutions that propelled her business to new heights. Surveys conducted within her organization indicated a marked increase in employee satisfaction, creativity, and overall productivity—proof that reducing digital distractions can foster an environment ripe for personal and professional growth.

The Ripple Effect of Personal Growth

The implications of personal growth through digital minimalism extend far beyond the individual. As we cultivate meaningful relationships, foster creativity, and clarify our goals, a ripple effect ensues. The positive impact of one person's mindful technology usage can inspire others to reconsider their own relationship with digital tools, driving a cultural shift towards a more intentional, sustainable way of living.

Encouragingly, mental health professionals advocate for the strategies of digital minimalism as part of a holistic approach to well-being. The incorporation of mindfulness practices—often intrinsic to the digital minimalism philosophy—further amplifies personal growth by promoting greater self-awareness. Techniques such as meditation and reflective journaling offer individuals the opportunity to process their experiences, deepen their understanding of self, and enhance personal development journeys.

Conclusion

Embracing digital minimalism is a transformative path toward personal growth—one that cultivates clarity, focus, and purpose. The evidence is clear: by intentionally reducing digital noise, we open ourselves to greater well-being and fulfillment. As you reflect on your own digital habits, consider how adopting a minimalist approach may foster the personal growth you have been seeking. It is time to reclaim your time and attention, and in doing so, unlock a fulfilling and enriching life filled with authentic connections, deep focus, and unyielding curiosity. The journey starts now—let digital minimalism guide you toward realizing your fullest potential.

XIV
Digital Detox: Is It Right for You?

In the ever-thrumming rhythm of our digital lives, the concept of a "digital detox" emerges as a compelling solution for those yearning to reclaim their time, attention, and mental clarity. This chapter dives into the nuanced understanding of what a digital detox encompasses, the potential benefits it can bring, and essential steps to ensure its success—integral for anyone ready to embark on this transformative journey.

What is Digital Detox?

A digital detox is a deliberate, temporary cessation from digital devices and the online world, intended to reset your habits and improve mental well-being. Studies show that excessive screen time can lead to increased anxiety, depression, and stress, with one research finding that those who spend more than two hours per day on digital devices are at a heightened risk for mental health issues (Twenge, 2017). In contrast, participants in digital detox programs report significant decreases in feelings of anxiety and a notable improvement in mood and overall well-being (Sweeney et al., 2020).

It isn't merely a break; it's an opportunity to foster deeper human connections and promote self-reflection. Dr. David Greenfield, an expert in behavioral technology, states, "When individuals take a break from technology, they can engage more with their environment, work through emotions, and reconnect with what truly matters."

The Potential Benefits of Digital Detox

1. **Improved Mental Clarity**: The constant barrage of notifications and information overload can lead to mental fog. An unequivocal benefit of stepping back from technology is mental clarity; research shows a strong connection between reduced screen time and improved cognitive functioning (Kuhl et al., 2021).

2. **Enhanced Relationships**: A digital detox can transform your interactions with others. A Stanford study revealed that face-to-face interactions foster deeper connections and understanding compared to online communications (Kosslyn et al., 2020). By unplugging, you can engage fully with those around you, driving meaningful conversations and connections.

3. **Rediscovery of Hobbies**: In reclaiming your time, you rediscover passions that may have languished under the weight of notifications and endless scrolling. Engaging in analog hobbies has been shown to enhance creativity and reduce stress (Niemann et al., 2019).

4. **Strengthened Focus**: The dopamine-driven distractions of digital devices splinter our attention. A study from the University of California found that multitasking can reduce productivity by as much as 40% (Mark et al., 2008). Coming back to a tech-free state allows for deeper focus and productivity.

Steps for Planning a Successful Digital Detox

1. **Define Your Intentions**: Begin by reflecting on what you seek to achieve through this detox. Is it clarity, connection, or perhaps a better work-life balance? Setting clear intentions can lend purpose to your journey.

2. **Establish a Timeline**: Whether a weekend, a week, or longer, determining a specific period can create a structure for your detox. Research shows that even short-term detoxes can have significant benefits (Hunsinger et al., 2021).

3. **Inform Your Circle**: Analog communication channels matter. Let friends, family, and colleagues know about your detox plan so they can support your journey and refrain from digital distractions during your time away.

4. **Set Boundaries**: Define what constitutes essential versus non-essential digital interactions. For example, work-related emails may be necessary, but scrolling through social feeds likely isn't.

5. **Engage in Substitute Activities**: Prepare a list of analog activities—reading, journaling, hiking—

that you can turn to in place of your usual digital habits. The goal is to cultivate engagement and so you can channel your energy into these enrichments.

Reflecting on the Experience

Post-detox reflection is critical. Consider journaling about your feelings, thoughts, and experiences during your digital hiatus. Were you surprised by any realizations? Did you find it difficult, or did you embrace the peace? Reflective practices can enhance self-awareness and solidify the positive impacts of the detox.

Moreover, the reintegration of digital tools must be strategic. Instead of returning to the same habits, ask yourself—"Which tools align with my goals?" Reintroducing technology with newfound mindfulness allows for a more intentional relationship moving forward.

Conclusion

When we step back from the digital chaos, we gain newfound perspectives and prioritize what truly adds value to our lives. A digital detox is more than just time away from screens; it is a chance to recalibrate, reconnect, and reclaim our attention in an ever-connected world. As you consider embarking on this journey, remember the potential rewards: mental clarity, enriched relationships, and a fortified sense of self. Allow the clarity of mind achieved through a digital detox to guide you towards a more intentional engagement with the technology that remains in your life, leading, ultimately, to a more fulfilling existence.

By embracing a digital detox, you pave the way for deeper awareness and the cultivation of a life where technology serves you—not the other way around. Isn't it time to take the plunge?

XV
Sharing Your Journey with Others

In a world saturated with notifications and digital noise, the journey toward digital minimalism can often feel isolating. However, sharing your experiences and insights not only helps you reinforce your commitment but can also cultivate a supportive community that inspires collective growth. By opening up conversations about your digital minimalist lifestyle, you encourage others to reflect on their technology use and explore meaningful alternatives.

Why Share Your Journey?

The Power of Influence Studies have consistently shown that social influence is a powerful motivator for behavior change. A 2017 study published in the journal *Nature Communications* illustrated that individuals were more likely to adopt behaviors modeled by their peers, emphasizing the importance of collective practice. When you share your journey into digital minimalism, you are not just recounting personal experiences;

you are potentially inspiring your friends and family to evaluate their own relationships with technology.

Creating Community Connections Research from the *American Psychological Association* highlights that community connections significantly impact mental well-being. Engaging in discussions about digital minimalism can forge deeper relationships and foster a sense of belonging. The shared goal of reducing digital clutter becomes a common ground for connection, enabling people to celebrate small victories together.

Tips for Discussing Digital Minimalism

1. **Be Open and Relatable**
   Start by sharing your struggles and successes. When you present your journey authentically, it gets others to relate and engage in dialogue. For instance, mention specific challenges you faced, like the allure of social media, and how you overcame them.

2. **Use Data and Examples**
   Ground your conversations in scientific evidence and real-life examples to highlight the benefits of digital minimalism. Mention that studies indicate excessive screen time correlates with rising anxiety and depression rates (Twenge et al., 2017). Use metrics from your own life: perhaps reducing your daily screen time led to more fulfilling personal interactions or heightened productivity levels at work.

3. **Encourage Reflection**

Ask leading questions that prompt reflection among those you talk to. For example, "Have you noticed how much time we all spend scrolling through our phones?" These questions create a sense of self-evaluation, leading to more meaningful discussions.

4. **Host Digital Minimalism Gatherings**
   Organizing a casual meet-up or workshop can create a supportive environment for discussion. Whether it's a book club focusing on digital minimalism or simply an invite for coffee without phones, these gatherings encourage shared exploration of pathways toward minimalism.

5. **Utilize Social Media Mindfully**
   While you may be practicing digital minimalism, showcasing essential insights via social media in a measured way can still be beneficial. Share your journey, not with the intention of garnering likes, but to relay thought-provoking content that sparks discussion. A study from *Harvard Business Review* found that sharing personal stories (especially struggles) can have a profound impact on audience engagement and connection.

Encouraging Others to Join the Movement

The goal of digital minimalism is not merely personal; it is about collective awareness and change.

1. **Lead by Example**
   Your lifestyle choices stand as a testament to the benefits of digital minimalism. Embrace and express the joy found in real-life interactions, analog

hobbies, and focused work sessions. Your actions will inevitably speak louder than words.

2. **Share Resources and Tools**
Provide books, articles, and podcasts that offer insights into digital minimalism. Resources like Cal Newport's *Digital Minimalism* can be a strong starting point for those unfamiliar with the philosophy. Research from *Pew Research Center* in 2019 found that sharing thoughtful content fosters greater understanding and awareness among social circles.

3. **Support Group Formation**

Initiate or join a local group focused on digital minimalism. Such groups create forums for shared experiences, accountability, and motivation, reinforcing commitments in a world full of distractions.

4. **Address Misconceptions**
Be prepared to counter common misconceptions surrounding digital minimalism, such as the idea that it means completely abandoning technology. Discuss how it is rather about intentionality. A balance can nurture healthier tech habits without sacrificing connectivity and convenience.

Creating Supportive Communities

As you navigate through your journey, consider the long-term impact of fostering communities around digital minimalism. A 2020 survey conducted by the *Digital Marketing Institute* found that 85% of respondents feel more positive and fulfilled when part of a supportive group. This statistic underscores the innate human desire for connection and support in achieving personal goals.

Joining forces not only strengthens your commitment but amplifies your influence, allowing digital minimalism to become a shared philosophy in your circle. Invite conversation, encourage introspection, and lead with empathy as you share your journey.

In conclusion, discussing your path towards digital minimalism opens doors to influence and create connections that can help others embark on their journeys. This ripple effect can lead to a broader, more informed dialogue about the ethical and thoughtful use of technology, ultimately fostering a community that thrives on intentional living. Emphasize the message that reclaiming time and attention from technology is not a solitary endeavor but a movement that benefits everyone.

XVI
The Future of Digital Minimalism

The digital landscape is in constant flux, evolving more rapidly than we can often comprehend. As we stand on the precipice of the next technological revolution, it is vital to consider what this means for the philosophy of digital minimalism. How will digital minimalism adapt to the advancements that shape our day-to-day technology usage? What opportunities and challenges lie ahead? The answers to these questions are not just speculative; they could very well define the quality of our digital lives in the years to come.

Trends Shaping the Digital Landscape

Recent studies indicate that we are witnessing a significant seismic shift in how technology is integrated into daily living. A report from *Pew Research Center* outlines that nearly 60% of American adults feel overwhelmed by the breadth and speed of technology change. As a response, many are turning towards practices that allow them to reclaim control over their digital interactions, encapsulated in the philosophy of digital minimalism.

Not only is this observable in anecdotal evidence, but also in solid data showing increased engagement in digital detoxes and a growing demand for products that prioritize user well-being through reduced screen-time features.

With the proliferation of Artificial Intelligence (AI) and the Internet of Things (IoT), we must critique how these technologies will fit within our lives. A study published in *Nature* warns that escalating screen time and the pressures of constant connectivity contribute to anxiety and depression. However, it also suggests that leveraging AI can help tailor our digital environments to foster mindfulness and intentional engagement. With smart devices learning our habits, they could help us manage our screen time more effectively if approached with a mindset that adheres to minimalism principles.

How Digital Minimalism Can Evolve with Technology

At its core, digital minimalism is about intentionality and awareness. This philosophy can serve as a framework to guide our interactions with ever-increasing technological advancements. The advent of augmented reality (AR) and virtual reality (VR) technologies, for example, may initially seem counterproductive to minimalism—after all, extended uses of these devices could lead to greater digital overwhelm. However, by applying minimalism principles to their use, we could create more meaningful experiences around learning, relaxation, and connection. Research from *Journal of Virtual Reality* shows that participants using VR for educational purposes reported heightened engagement and retained more information—a clear indication that thoughtfully designed technology can enrich our lives when used with intent.

Moreover, as the ante is raised on consumer technology, ethical considerations surrounding data privacy, technological addiction, and environmental impact will necessitate a renewed commitment to digital minimalism. A report from the *Global Digital Policy Institute* highlights the ethical dilemmas posed by tech firms prioritizing profit over user well-being. Digital minimalists can advocate for transparency and ethical practices as part of their mandate, encouraging companies that prioritize the user experience and sustainable practices.

Predictions and Hopes for Sustainable Digital Living

The future of digital minimalism is not just about reducing our technological footprint. It offers a hopeful vision for a balanced coexistence with technology, where we harness its potential without compromising our mental health and relationships. The desire for sustainability is rising among consumers, prompting companies to rethink their strategies and focus on more ethical production and design practices. According to a survey by *McKinsey*, 66% of consumers are willing to pay more for sustainable products, indicating a collective shift towards values-driven consumption. Digital minimalists can lead this charge, advocating for tech that aligns with a sustainable lifestyle—both environmentally and socially.

Additionally, with the rise of remote work and online education, we are forced to reassess how technology assists—rather than dictates—our productivity and learning. A study in *Harvard Business Review* found that employees who set strict boundaries around their digital availability reported increased job satisfaction and reduced burnout. This insight underscores the importance of incorporating digital minimalism into our work-life balance moving forward.

In summary, the future of digital minimalism is both exciting and necessary. As technology continues to weave its way into the very fabric of our daily lives, we must defend our agency and commit ourselves to a thoughtful approach. By embracing this ideology, we not only enhance our well-being but also contribute to a more ethical and sustainable technological landscape. Together, let us navigate this new digital world—relentlessly pursuing the principles of intentionality, mindfulness, and connection that digital minimalism champions. The time has come for the next phase of our digital journey; let us make it meaningful.

XVII
Case Studies of Digital Minimalism

In an age where our screens dictate so much of our daily existence, stories from the frontlines of digital minimalism serve as powerful testimonials of its transformative potential. This chapter aims to explore inspiring case studies of individuals who have embraced digital minimalism, showcasing their unique journeys, the challenges they encountered, and the profound insights they gained along the way. Through these narratives, we will illustrate not only the benefits of intentional technology use but also the actionable takeaways that can empower others to embark on a similar path.

Case Study 1: The Corporate Executive

Meet Sarah, a corporate executive who began feeling overwhelmed by her digital commitments. Working long hours meant that her smartphone was always at hand, and that constant connectivity blurred the lines between work and personal life. A study published in the *Journal of Occupational Health Psychology* found that "excessive smartphone use correlates with increased stress levels and decreased life satisfaction." Sarah found herself in that statistic.

Realizing that her phone was more of a distraction than a tool, Sarah turned to digital minimalism. First, she conducted a digital audit—evaluating her apps and rearranging her notifications. Instead of checking her emails every few minutes, she committed to specific times for digital communication. As a result, her productivity soared, and she reported a staggering 25% increase in her output within the first month.

The most significant change, however, was in her personal life. By reducing her screen time, Sarah rediscovered her passion for painting and started attending art classes. "I realized how much I had neglected my hobbies," she reflected. "Without the digital noise, I could hear my own thoughts again."

Case Study 2: The College Student

Jake, a college junior, found himself in a spiral of endless scrolling on social media, which consumed hours each day. A 2022 study from the University of Pennsylvania found that students who limited their social media usage reported improvements in their well-being and reduced anxiety. Feeling the pressure of his academic performance coupled with diminished mental health, Jake decided to embrace digital minimalism.

He initiated a "social media cleanse," eliminating all but one platform—Instagram, where he followed accounts that inspired him academically instead of mindlessly scrolling. Jake also began substituting digital distractions with physical activities like jogging and hanging out with friends without screens.

The results were astounding. Jake's grades improved by entire letter grades, and he also reported feeling more fulfilled and connected to his peers during in-person interactions. He underscores this in his own words: "When I stopped using social media as a crutch, I found genuine connections in the real world."

Case Study 3: The Stay-at-Home Parent

Linda, a mother of three young children, felt that technology was encroaching on precious family time. Research from the *American Psychological Association* indicates that excessive screen time can disrupt family dynamics, leading to decreased interaction and bonding. A wake-up call convinced her to intentionally reduce her screen time.

Linda began implementing "tech-free zones" at home, specifically during family dinners and playtime. She also replaced mindless browsing with reading books to her children and engaging them in outdoor activities.

Within weeks, Linda and her family experienced a tangible shift in their dynamic. She documented a 40% increase in quality family time and a noticeable improvement in her children's behavior and attention spans. "We started to connect in ways I never thought possible," Linda shared. "It was like rediscovering my family again."

Actionable Takeaways

The journeys of Sarah, Jake, and Linda illustrate a vital truth: embracing digital minimalism is not solely an individual endeavor but a communal shift toward more intentional living. Each story provides valuable insights that can inspire others on their path to reducing the digital clutter in their lives:

1. **Conduct a Digital Audit**: Regularly assess the apps and tools you use. Ask yourself: Does this enhance my life? By shedding unnecessary digital weight, as Sarah did, you create space for more meaningful activities.

2. **Set Boundaries**: Like Jake's college experiment, establish specific times for technology use. This practice fosters an environment conducive to focused work and healthy relationships.

3. **Create Tech-Free Zones**: Implement areas or times in your life where screens are not allowed, as Linda did. This allows you to cultivate authentic connections with those around you.

4. **Rediscover Hobbies and Interests**: Use the time saved from reduced screen time to explore passions and hobbies. The personal growth that comes from engaging in meaningful activities can lead to a deeper sense of fulfillment.

5. **Engage with Community**: Share your goals and experiences with others. Encourage family and friends to join you in this minimalistic approach to technology, creating a supportive network.

As we analyze these case studies, it becomes clear that the path toward digital minimalism offers more than mere disconnection from devices; it presents an opportunity to reclaim time, strengthen relationships, and enhance personal growth. In a world overwhelmed by digital distractions, these inspiring stories illuminate the path to a more intentional, fulfilling life. Embrace the simplicity, and your journey toward a meaningful existence may just be a mindful decision away.

XVIII
Conclusion: Reclaiming Your Time and Attention

In a world saturated with incessant notifications, swirling feeds, and perpetual digital engagement, the philosophy of digital minimalism emerges as a beacon of hope. It invites us to rethink our relationship with technology, urging us to reclaim our time and attention—a currency more precious than gold. As you embark upon this journey of intentionality, the question looms: what will you choose to prioritize?

Recent studies illuminate the pressing need for a mindful approach to technology. Research published in the journal *Psychological Science* indicates that excessive screen time is correlated with increased rates of anxiety and depression among adolescents. A survey conducted by the American Psychological Association found that 61% of adults believe that social media negatively impacts their mental health. Faced with these statistics, it is clear that the continued unreflective use of technology can hold us captive, hindering our pursuit of happiness and fulfillment.

Digital minimalism confronts these challenges by advocating for intentional technology use—questioning whether our digital tools genuinely align with our values and enhance our lives. It's not about abandoning technology altogether but about being discerning in its application. A 2020 study from the Pew Research Center revealed that parents who actively managed their children's screen time reported higher family cohesion and improved communication. This suggests that as we refine our own digital habits, we can guide those around us to a healthier relationship with technology.

Moreover, one of the most significant shifts achievable through digital minimalism is the reduction of screen time. Evidence from a study published in *JAMA Surgery* demonstrated that patients who limited their screen time experienced significantly improved mental well-being, with reductions in anxiety and depression levels. By consciously choosing to disconnect from our devices, we liberate time for relationships, personal projects, and even mental clarity.

As we explored in earlier chapters, embracing analog alternatives opens a world rich in experiences previously overshadowed by screens. A fascinating study in the journal *Psychological Science* revealed that individuals who engaged in face-to-face interactions reported higher life satisfaction compared to those who primarily communicated digitally. By replacing the thumb scroll with page turns and text messages with heartfelt conversations, we enrich our social fabric and foster deeper connections.

Digital decluttering is another vital cornerstone of digital minimalism and its impact cannot be understated. Findings from the International Journal of Human-Computer Studies imply that a cluttered digital environment increases our cognitive load, leading to stress and decreased productivity. Decluttering your digital spaces not only creates a streamlined environment but also generates mental clarity, allowing your mind to focus on what truly matters.

Furthermore, by honing our focus and productivity, we tap into our full potential. A report by the Stanford Graduate School of Business revealed that multitasking can lead to a 40% decrease in productivity, underscoring the value of deep work—a principle championed by the digital minimalist lifestyle. With intentional practices in place, we create an opportunity for profound creativity and innovation, along with enhanced professional performance.

Importantly, the rewards of digital minimalism extend to our relationships, as minimizing digital communication encourages more meaningful in-person interactions. Studies have consistently shown that strong personal relationships are linked to improved mental health and longevity. By honoring our interpersonal connections, we cultivate a supportive community that nourishes our souls.

Ultimately, digital minimalism prompts us to reconsider our consumption and the ethical implications of technology use. As we engage in meaningful conversations around sustainability and the environmental impact of tech waste, we align our choices with our values. A growing body of research, such as that conducted by Greenpeace, shows that sustainable technology practices not only benefit the planet but also galvanize community involvement.

In conclusion, digital minimalism is not merely an approach to technology; it's a lifestyle designed to cultivate mindfulness, intentionality, and fulfillment. It offers a pathway toward reclaiming our time and attention in this relentless digital age. The challenge that remains is for you to take up the mantle and make the conscious choice to engage differently with your digital tools.

You have the power to reshape your narrative. Embrace the principles of digital minimalism, initiate your action plan, and witness the transformative potential that unfolds when you intentionally live with technology rather than in servitude to it. Together, let us cultivate a future where technology enchants rather than encumbers, where you can find clarity, connection, and purpose in a tech-driven world. Your journey towards a more intentional life starts today—will you take the first step?

www.ingramcontent.com/pod-product-compliance
Lightning Source LLC
Chambersburg PA
CBHW030446220526
45464CB00006B/2429